$500 in
Savings c

$2 $3 $4 $5 $6

$7 $8 $9 $10 $11

$12 $13 $14 $15 $16

$17 $18 $19 $20 $21

$22 $23 $24 $25 $26

$27 $28 $29 $30 $31

Notes: _____
_____
_____
_____

$500 in 30 Days

Savings challenge

$2	$3	$4	$5	$6
$7	$8	$9	$10	$11
$12	$13	$14	$15	$16
$17	$18	$19	$20	$21
$22	$23	$24	$25	$26
$27	$28	$29	$30	$31

Notes: _____
_____
_____

$500 in 30 Days

Savings challenge

$2	$3	$4	$5	$6
$7	$8	$9	$10	$11
$12	$13	$14	$15	$16
$17	$18	$19	$20	$21
$22	$23	$24	$25	$26
$27	$28	$29	$30	$31

Notes:

$500 in 30 Days

Savings challenge

$2	$3	$4	$5	$6
$7	$8	$9	$10	$11
$12	$13	$14	$15	$16
$17	$18	$19	$20	$21
$22	$23	$24	$25	$26
$27	$28	$29	$30	$31

Notes: _____
_____
_____
_____

$500 in 30 Days

Savings challenge

$2 $3 $4 $5 $6

$7 $8 $9 $10 $11

$12 $13 $14 $15 $16

$17 $18 $19 $20 $21

$22 $23 $24 $25 $26

$27 $28 $29 $30 $31

Notes: _____
_____
_____

$500 in 30 Days

Savings challenge

$2	$3	$4	$5	$6
$7	$8	$9	$10	$11
$12	$13	$14	$15	$16
$17	$18	$19	$20	$21
$22	$23	$24	$25	$26
$27	$28	$29	$30	$31

Notes: _____
_____
_____

$500 in 30 Days

Savings challenge

$2	$3	$4	$5	$6
$7	$8	$9	$10	$11
$12	$13	$14	$15	$16
$17	$18	$19	$20	$21
$22	$23	$24	$25	$26
$27	$28	$29	$30	$31

Notes: _____
_____
_____

$500 in 30 Days
Savings challenge

$2 $3 $4 $5 $6

$7 $8 $9 $10 $11

$12 $13 $14 $15 $16

$17 $18 $19 $20 $21

$22 $23 $24 $25 $26

$27 $28 $29 $30 $31

Notes: _____
_____
_____
_____

$500 in 30 Days

Savings challenge

$2	$3	$4	$5	$6
$7	$8	$9	$10	$11
$12	$13	$14	$15	$16
$17	$18	$19	$20	$21
$22	$23	$24	$25	$26
$27	$28	$29	$30	$31

Notes: _____

_____

_____

$500 in 30 Days

Savings challenge

$2	$3	$4	$5	$6
$7	$8	$9	$10	$11
$12	$13	$14	$15	$16
$17	$18	$19	$20	$21
$22	$23	$24	$25	$26
$27	$28	$29	$30	$31

Notes: _____
_____
_____
_____

$500 in 30 Days

Savings challenge

$2	$3	$4	$5	$6
$7	$8	$9	$10	$11
$12	$13	$14	$15	$16
$17	$18	$19	$20	$21
$22	$23	$24	$25	$26
$27	$28	$29	$30	$31

Notes: _____

_____

_____

$500 in 30 Days

Savings challenge

$2	$3	$4	$5	$6
$7	$8	$9	$10	$11
$12	$13	$14	$15	$16
$17	$18	$19	$20	$21
$22	$23	$24	$25	$26
$27	$28	$29	$30	$31

Notes: _____
_____
_____
_____

$500 in 30 Days

Savings challenge

$2	$3	$4	$5	$6
$7	$8	$9	$10	$11
$12	$13	$14	$15	$16
$17	$18	$19	$20	$21
$22	$23	$24	$25	$26
$27	$28	$29	$30	$31

Notes: _____

_____

_____

$500 in 30 Days

Savings challenge

$2	$3	$4	$5	$6
$7	$8	$9	$10	$11
$12	$13	$14	$15	$16
$17	$18	$19	$20	$21
$22	$23	$24	$25	$26
$27	$28	$29	$30	$31

Notes: _____
_____
_____

$500 in 30 Days

Savings challenge

$2	$3	$4	$5	$6
$7	$8	$9	$10	$11
$12	$13	$14	$15	$16
$17	$18	$19	$20	$21
$22	$23	$24	$25	$26
$27	$28	$29	$30	$31

Notes: _____
_____
_____
_____

$500 in 30 Days

Savings challenge

$2	$3	$4	$5	$6
$7	$8	$9	$10	$11
$12	$13	$14	$15	$16
$17	$18	$19	$20	$21
$22	$23	$24	$25	$26
$27	$28	$29	$30	$31

Notes: _____
_____
_____
_____

$500 in 30 Days

Savings challenge

$2	$3	$4	$5	$6
$7	$8	$9	$10	$11
$12	$13	$14	$15	$16
$17	$18	$19	$20	$21
$22	$23	$24	$25	$26
$27	$28	$29	$30	$31

Notes: _____

_____

_____

$500 in 30 Days

Savings challenge

$2	$3	$4	$5	$6
$7	$8	$9	$10	$11
$12	$13	$14	$15	$16
$17	$18	$19	$20	$21
$22	$23	$24	$25	$26
$27	$28	$29	$30	$31

Notes: _____

_____

_____

_____

$500 in 30 Days

Savings challenge

$2	$3	$4	$5	$6
$7	$8	$9	$10	$11
$12	$13	$14	$15	$16
$17	$18	$19	$20	$21
$22	$23	$24	$25	$26
$27	$28	$29	$30	$31

Notes: _____
_____
_____
_____

$500 in 30 Days

Savings challenge

$2 $3 $4 $5 $6

$7 $8 $9 $10 $11

$12 $13 $14 $15 $16

$17 $18 $19 $20 $21

$22 $23 $24 $25 $26

$27 $28 $29 $30 $31

Notes: _____

$500 in 30 Days

Savings challenge

$2	$3	$4	$5	$6
$7	$8	$9	$10	$11
$12	$13	$14	$15	$16
$17	$18	$19	$20	$21
$22	$23	$24	$25	$26
$27	$28	$29	$30	$31

Notes: _____
_____
_____
_____

$500 in 30 Days

Savings challenge

$2	$3	$4	$5	$6
$7	$8	$9	$10	$11
$12	$13	$14	$15	$16
$17	$18	$19	$20	$21
$22	$23	$24	$25	$26
$27	$28	$29	$30	$31

Notes: _____
_____
_____
_____

$500 in 30 Days

Savings challenge

$2	$3	$4	$5	$6
$7	$8	$9	$10	$11
$12	$13	$14	$15	$16
$17	$18	$19	$20	$21
$22	$23	$24	$25	$26
$27	$28	$29	$30	$31

Notes: _____
_____
_____

$500 in 30 Days

Savings challenge

$2 $3 $4 $5 $6

$7 $8 $9 $10 $11

$12 $13 $14 $15 $16

$17 $18 $19 $20 $21

$22 $23 $24 $25 $26

$27 $28 $29 $30 $31

Notes:

$500 in 30 Days

Savings challenge

$2	$3	$4	$5	$6
$7	$8	$9	$10	$11
$12	$13	$14	$15	$16
$17	$18	$19	$20	$21
$22	$23	$24	$25	$26
$27	$28	$29	$30	$31

Notes: _____

_____

_____

$500 in 30 Days

Savings challenge

$2	$3	$4	$5	$6
$7	$8	$9	$10	$11
$12	$13	$14	$15	$16
$17	$18	$19	$20	$21
$22	$23	$24	$25	$26
$27	$28	$29	$30	$31

Notes: _____
_____
_____
_____

$500 in 30 Days
Savings challenge

$2	$3	$4	$5	$6
$7	$8	$9	$10	$11
$12	$13	$14	$15	$16
$17	$18	$19	$20	$21
$22	$23	$24	$25	$26
$27	$28	$29	$30	$31

Notes: _____

_____

_____

$500 in 30 Days

Savings challenge

$2	$3	$4	$5	$6
$7	$8	$9	$10	$11
$12	$13	$14	$15	$16
$17	$18	$19	$20	$21
$22	$23	$24	$25	$26
$27	$28	$29	$30	$31

Notes: _____
_____
_____
_____

$500 in 30 Days
Savings challenge

$2	$3	$4	$5	$6
$7	$8	$9	$10	$11
$12	$13	$14	$15	$16
$17	$18	$19	$20	$21
$22	$23	$24	$25	$26
$27	$28	$29	$30	$31

Notes: _____
_____
_____

$500 in 30 Days

Savings challenge

$2 $3 $4 $5 $6

$7 $8 $9 $10 $11

$12 $13 $14 $15 $16

$17 $18 $19 $20 $21

$22 $23 $24 $25 $26

$27 $28 $29 $30 $31

Notes:

$300 in 40 Days

Savings challenge

$5	$6	$9	$13	$15
$12	$23	$7	$24	$2
$14	$16	Free	$4	$10
$18	$11	$19	$21	$17
$20	$8	$1	$3	$22

Notes: _____
_____
_____

$300 in 40 Days

Savings challenge

$5	$6	$9	$13	$15
$12	$23	$7	$24	$2
$14	$16	Free	$4	$10
$18	$11	$19	$21	$17
$20	$8	$1	$3	$22

Notes: _____
_____
_____

$300 in 40 Days

Savings challenge

$5	$6	$9	$13	$15
$12	$23	$7	$24	$2
$14	$16	Free	$4	$10
$18	$11	$19	$21	$17
$20	$8	$1	$3	$22

Notes: _____
_____
_____

$300 in 40 Days

Savings challenge

$5	$6	$9	$13	$15
$12	$23	$7	$24	$2
$14	$16	Free	$4	$10
$18	$11	$19	$21	$17
$20	$8	$1	$3	$22

Notes:

$300 in 40 Days

Savings challenge

$5	$6	$9	$13	$15
$12	$23	$7	$24	$2
$14	$16	Free	$4	$10
$18	$11	$19	$21	$17
$20	$8	$1	$3	$22

Notes: _____
_____
_____

$300 in 40 Days

Savings challenge

$5	$6	$9	$13	$15
$12	$23	$7	$24	$2
$14	$16	Free	$4	$10
$18	$11	$19	$21	$17
$20	$8	$1	$3	$22

Notes:

$300 in 40 Days

Savings challenge

$5	$6	$9	$13	$15
$12	$23	$7	$24	$2
$14	$16	Free	$4	$10
$18	$11	$19	$21	$17
$20	$8	$1	$3	$22

Notes: _____

_____

_____

$300 in 40 Days

Savings challenge

$5	$6	$9	$13	$15
$12	$23	$7	$24	$2
$14	$16	Free	$4	$10
$18	$11	$19	$21	$17
$20	$8	$1	$3	$22

Notes: _____
_____
_____

$300 in 40 Days

Savings challenge

$5	$6	$9	$13	$15
$12	$23	$7	$24	$2
$14	$16	Free	$4	$10
$18	$11	$19	$21	$17
$20	$8	$1	$3	$22

Notes: _____
_____
_____

$300 in 40 Days

Savings challenge

$5	$6	$9	$13	$15
$12	$23	$7	$24	$2
$14	$16	Free	$4	$10
$18	$11	$19	$21	$17
$20	$8	$1	$3	$22

Notes: _____
_____
_____
_____

$300 in 40 Days

Savings challenge

$5	$6	$9	$13	$15
$12	$23	$7	$24	$2
$14	$16	Free	$4	$10
$18	$11	$19	$21	$17
$20	$8	$1	$3	$22

Notes: _____
_____
_____

$300 in 40 Days

Savings challenge

$5	$6	$9	$13	$15
$12	$23	$7	$24	$2
$14	$16	Free	$4	$10
$18	$11	$19	$21	$17
$20	$8	$1	$3	$22

Notes: _____
_____
_____

$300 in 40 Days

Savings challenge

$5	$6	$9	$13	$15
$12	$23	$7	$24	$2
$14	$16	Free	$4	$10
$18	$11	$19	$21	$17
$20	$8	$1	$3	$22

Notes: _____
_____
_____
_____

$300 in 40 Days

Savings challenge

$5	$6	$9	$13	$15
$12	$23	$7	$24	$2
$14	$16	Free	$4	$10
$18	$11	$19	$21	$17
$20	$8	$1	$3	$22

Notes: _____
_____
_____

$300 in 40 Days
Savings challenge

$5	$6	$9	$13	$15
$12	$23	$7	$24	$2
$14	$16	Free	$4	$10
$18	$11	$19	$21	$17
$20	$8	$1	$3	$22

Notes: _____
_____
_____

$300 in 40 Days

Savings challenge

$5	$6	$9	$13	$15
$12	$23	$7	$24	$2
$14	$16	Free	$4	$10
$18	$11	$19	$21	$17
$20	$8	$1	$3	$22

Notes: _____
_____
_____
_____

$300 in 40 Days

Savings challenge

$5	$6	$9	$13	$15
$12	$23	$7	$24	$2
$14	$16	Free	$4	$10
$18	$11	$19	$21	$17
$20	$8	$1	$3	$22

Notes:

$300 in 40 Days

Savings challenge

$5	$6	$9	$13	$15
$12	$23	$7	$24	$2
$14	$16	Free	$4	$10
$18	$11	$19	$21	$17
$20	$8	$1	$3	$22

Notes: _____
_____
_____

$300 in 40 Days

Savings challenge

$5	$6	$9	$13	$15
$12	$23	$7	$24	$2
$14	$16	Free	$4	$10
$18	$11	$19	$21	$17
$20	$8	$1	$3	$22

Notes: _____
_____
_____
_____

$300 in 40 Days

Savings challenge

$5	$6	$9	$13	$15
$12	$23	$7	$24	$2
$14	$16	Free	$4	$10
$18	$11	$19	$21	$17
$20	$8	$1	$3	$22

Notes: _____
_____
_____

$300 in 40 Days

Savings challenge

$5	$6	$9	$13	$15
$12	$23	$7	$24	$2
$14	$16	Free	$4	$10
$18	$11	$19	$21	$17
$20	$8	$1	$3	$22

Notes: _____
_____
_____

$300 in 40 Days

Savings challenge

$5	$6	$9	$13	$15
$12	$23	$7	$24	$2
$14	$16	Free	$4	$10
$18	$11	$19	$21	$17
$20	$8	$1	$3	$22

Notes: _____
_____
_____

$300 in 40 Days
Savings challenge

$5	$6	$9	$13	$15
$12	$23	$7	$24	$2
$14	$16	Free	$4	$10
$18	$11	$19	$21	$17
$20	$8	$1	$3	$22

Notes: _____
_____
_____
_____

$300 in 40 Days

Savings challenge

$5	$6	$9	$13	$15
$12	$23	$7	$24	$2
$14	$16	Free	$4	$10
$18	$11	$19	$21	$17
$20	$8	$1	$3	$22

Notes:

$300 in 40 Days

Savings challenge

$5	$6	$9	$13	$15
$12	$23	$7	$24	$2
$14	$16	Free	$4	$10
$18	$11	$19	$21	$17
$20	$8	$1	$3	$22

Notes: _____
_____
_____

$300 in 40 Days
Savings challenge

$5	$6	$9	$13	$15
$12	$23	$7	$24	$2
$14	$16	Free	$4	$10
$18	$11	$19	$21	$17
$20	$8	$1	$3	$22

Notes: _____
_____
_____

$300 in 40 Days

Savings challenge

$5	$6	$9	$13	$15
$12	$23	$7	$24	$2
$14	$16	Free	$4	$10
$18	$11	$19	$21	$17
$20	$8	$1	$3	$22

Notes: _____
_____
_____

$300 in 40 Days

Savings challenge

$5	$6	$9	$13	$15
$12	$23	$7	$24	$2
$14	$16	Free	$4	$10
$18	$11	$19	$21	$17
$20	$8	$1	$3	$22

Notes: _____
_____
_____
_____

$300 in 40 Days

Savings challenge

$5	$6	$9	$13	$15
$12	$23	$7	$24	$2
$14	$16	Free	$4	$10
$18	$11	$19	$21	$17
$20	$8	$1	$3	$22

Notes: _____
_____
_____
_____

$300 in 40 Days

Savings challenge

$5	$6	$9	$13	$15
$12	$23	$7	$24	$2
$14	$16	Free	$4	$10
$18	$11	$19	$21	$17
$20	$8	$1	$3	$22

Notes:

Road to save $ 1,000

In 3 months

3 MONTHS SAVINGS PLAN

Week 1	$77	☐
Week 2	$77	☐
Week 3	$77	☐
Week 4	$77	☐
Week 5	$77	☐
Week 6	$77	☐
Week 7	$77	☐
Week 8	$77	☐
Week 9	$77	☐
Week 10	$77	☐
Week 11	$77	☐
Week 12	$77	☐
Week 13	$77	☐

Notes: _____
_____
_____

Road to save $ 1,000

In 3 months

3 MONTHS SAVINGS PLAN

Week 1	$77	☐
Week 2	$77	☐
Week 3	$77	☐
Week 4	$77	☐
Week 5	$77	☐
Week 6	$77	☐
Week 7	$77	☐
Week 8	$77	☐
Week 9	$77	☐
Week 10	$77	☐
Week 11	$77	☐
Week 12	$77	☐
Week 13	$77	☐

Notes: _____
_____
_____

Road to save $ 1,000

In 3 months

3 MONTHS SAVINGS PLAN

Week 1	$77	☐
Week 2	$77	☐
Week 3	$77	☐
Week 4	$77	☐
Week 5	$77	☐
Week 6	$77	☐
Week 7	$77	☐
Week 8	$77	☐
Week 9	$77	☐
Week 10	$77	☐
Week 11	$77	☐
Week 12	$77	☐
Week 13	$77	☐

Notes: _____
_____
_____

Road to save $ 1,000

In 3 months

3 MONTHS SAVINGS PLAN

Week 1	$77	☐
Week 2	$77	☐
Week 3	$77	☐
Week 4	$77	☐
Week 5	$77	☐
Week 6	$77	☐
Week 7	$77	☐
Week 8	$77	☐
Week 9	$77	☐
Week 10	$77	☐
Week 11	$77	☐
Week 12	$77	☐
Week 13	$77	☐

Notes: _____
_____
_____

Road to save $ 1,000

In 3 months

3 MONTHS SAVINGS PLAN

Week 1	$77	☐
Week 2	$77	☐
Week 3	$77	☐
Week 4	$77	☐
Week 5	$77	☐
Week 6	$77	☐
Week 7	$77	☐
Week 8	$77	☐
Week 9	$77	☐
Week 10	$77	☐
Week 11	$77	☐
Week 12	$77	☐
Week 13	$77	☐

Notes: _____
_____
_____

Road to save $ 1,000

In 3 months

3 MONTHS SAVINGS PLAN

Week 1	$77	☐
Week 2	$77	☐
Week 3	$77	☐
Week 4	$77	☐
Week 5	$77	☐
Week 6	$77	☐
Week 7	$77	☐
Week 8	$77	☐
Week 9	$77	☐
Week 10	$77	☐
Week 11	$77	☐
Week 12	$77	☐
Week 13	$77	☐

Notes: _____
_____
_____

Road to save $ 1,000

In 3 months

3 MONTHS SAVINGS PLAN

Week 1	$77	☐
Week 2	$77	☐
Week 3	$77	☐
Week 4	$77	☐
Week 5	$77	☐
Week 6	$77	☐
Week 7	$77	☐
Week 8	$77	☐
Week 9	$77	☐
Week 10	$77	☐
Week 11	$77	☐
Week 12	$77	☐
Week 13	$77	☐

Notes: _____
_____
_____

Road to save $ 1,000

In 3 months

3 MONTHS SAVINGS PLAN

Week 1	$77	☐
Week 2	$77	☐
Week 3	$77	☐
Week 4	$77	☐
Week 5	$77	☐
Week 6	$77	☐
Week 7	$77	☐
Week 8	$77	☐
Week 9	$77	☐
Week 10	$77	☐
Week 11	$77	☐
Week 12	$77	☐
Week 13	$77	☐

Notes: _____
_____
_____

Road to save $ 1,000

In 3 months

3 MONTHS SAVINGS PLAN

Week 1	$77	☐
Week 2	$77	☐
Week 3	$77	☐
Week 4	$77	☐
Week 5	$77	☐
Week 6	$77	☐
Week 7	$77	☐
Week 8	$77	☐
Week 9	$77	☐
Week 10	$77	☐
Week 11	$77	☐
Week 12	$77	☐
Week 13	$77	☐

Notes: _____
_____
_____

Road to save $ 1,000

In 3 months

3 MONTHS SAVINGS PLAN

Week 1	$77	☐
Week 2	$77	☐
Week 3	$77	☐
Week 4	$77	☐
Week 5	$77	☐
Week 6	$77	☐
Week 7	$77	☐
Week 8	$77	☐
Week 9	$77	☐
Week 10	$77	☐
Week 11	$77	☐
Week 12	$77	☐
Week 13	$77	☐

Notes: _____
_____
_____

Road to save $ 1,000

In 3 months

3 MONTHS SAVINGS PLAN

Week 1	$77	☐
Week 2	$77	☐
Week 3	$77	☐
Week 4	$77	☐
Week 5	$77	☐
Week 6	$77	☐
Week 7	$77	☐
Week 8	$77	☐
Week 9	$77	☐
Week 10	$77	☐
Week 11	$77	☐
Week 12	$77	☐
Week 13	$77	☐

Notes: _____
_____
_____

Road to save $ 1,000

In 3 months

3 MONTHS SAVINGS PLAN

Week 1	$77	☐
Week 2	$77	☐
Week 3	$77	☐
Week 4	$77	☐
Week 5	$77	☐
Week 6	$77	☐
Week 7	$77	☐
Week 8	$77	☐
Week 9	$77	☐
Week 10	$77	☐
Week 11	$77	☐
Week 12	$77	☐
Week 13	$77	☐

Notes: _____
_____
_____

Road to save $ 1,000

In 3 months

3 MONTHS SAVINGS PLAN

Week 1	$77	☐
Week 2	$77	☐
Week 3	$77	☐
Week 4	$77	☐
Week 5	$77	☐
Week 6	$77	☐
Week 7	$77	☐
Week 8	$77	☐
Week 9	$77	☐
Week 10	$77	☐
Week 11	$77	☐
Week 12	$77	☐
Week 13	$77	☐

Notes: _____
_____
_____

Road to save $ 1,000

In 3 months

3 MONTHS SAVINGS PLAN

Week 1	$77	☐
Week 2	$77	☐
Week 3	$77	☐
Week 4	$77	☐
Week 5	$77	☐
Week 6	$77	☐
Week 7	$77	☐
Week 8	$77	☐
Week 9	$77	☐
Week 10	$77	☐
Week 11	$77	☐
Week 12	$77	☐
Week 13	$77	☐

Notes: _____
_____
_____

Road to save $ 1,000

In 3 months

3 MONTHS SAVINGS PLAN

Week 1	$77	☐
Week 2	$77	☐
Week 3	$77	☐
Week 4	$77	☐
Week 5	$77	☐
Week 6	$77	☐
Week 7	$77	☐
Week 8	$77	☐
Week 9	$77	☐
Week 10	$77	☐
Week 11	$77	☐
Week 12	$77	☐
Week 13	$77	☐

Notes:

Road to save $ 1,000

In 3 months

3 MONTHS SAVINGS PLAN

Week 1	$77	☐
Week 2	$77	☐
Week 3	$77	☐
Week 4	$77	☐
Week 5	$77	☐
Week 6	$77	☐
Week 7	$77	☐
Week 8	$77	☐
Week 9	$77	☐
Week 10	$77	☐
Week 11	$77	☐
Week 12	$77	☐
Week 13	$77	☐

Notes: _____
_____
_____

Road to save $ 1,000

In 3 months

3 MONTHS SAVINGS PLAN

Week 1	$77	☐
Week 2	$77	☐
Week 3	$77	☐
Week 4	$77	☐
Week 5	$77	☐
Week 6	$77	☐
Week 7	$77	☐
Week 8	$77	☐
Week 9	$77	☐
Week 10	$77	☐
Week 11	$77	☐
Week 12	$77	☐
Week 13	$77	☐

Notes:

Road to save $ 1,000

In 3 months

3 MONTHS SAVINGS PLAN

Week 1	$77	☐
Week 2	$77	☐
Week 3	$77	☐
Week 4	$77	☐
Week 5	$77	☐
Week 6	$77	☐
Week 7	$77	☐
Week 8	$77	☐
Week 9	$77	☐
Week 10	$77	☐
Week 11	$77	☐
Week 12	$77	☐
Week 13	$77	☐

Notes: _____
_____
_____
_____

Road to save $ 1,000

In 3 months

3 MONTHS SAVINGS PLAN

Week 1	$77	☐
Week 2	$77	☐
Week 3	$77	☐
Week 4	$77	☐
Week 5	$77	☐
Week 6	$77	☐
Week 7	$77	☐
Week 8	$77	☐
Week 9	$77	☐
Week 10	$77	☐
Week 11	$77	☐
Week 12	$77	☐
Week 13	$77	☐

Notes: _____
_____
_____

Road to save $ 1,000

In 3 months

3 MONTHS SAVINGS PLAN

Week 1	$77	☐
Week 2	$77	☐
Week 3	$77	☐
Week 4	$77	☐
Week 5	$77	☐
Week 6	$77	☐
Week 7	$77	☐
Week 8	$77	☐
Week 9	$77	☐
Week 10	$77	☐
Week 11	$77	☐
Week 12	$77	☐
Week 13	$77	☐

Notes: _____
_____
_____

Road to save $ 1,000

In 3 months

3 MONTHS SAVINGS PLAN

Week 1	$77	☐
Week 2	$77	☐
Week 3	$77	☐
Week 4	$77	☐
Week 5	$77	☐
Week 6	$77	☐
Week 7	$77	☐
Week 8	$77	☐
Week 9	$77	☐
Week 10	$77	☐
Week 11	$77	☐
Week 12	$77	☐
Week 13	$77	☐

Notes: _____
_____
_____

Road to save $ 1,000

In 3 months

3 MONTHS SAVINGS PLAN

Week 1	$77	☐
Week 2	$77	☐
Week 3	$77	☐
Week 4	$77	☐
Week 5	$77	☐
Week 6	$77	☐
Week 7	$77	☐
Week 8	$77	☐
Week 9	$77	☐
Week 10	$77	☐
Week 11	$77	☐
Week 12	$77	☐
Week 13	$77	☐

Notes: _____
_____
_____

Road to save $ 1,000

In 3 months

3 MONTHS SAVINGS PLAN

Week 1	$77	☐
Week 2	$77	☐
Week 3	$77	☐
Week 4	$77	☐
Week 5	$77	☐
Week 6	$77	☐
Week 7	$77	☐
Week 8	$77	☐
Week 9	$77	☐
Week 10	$77	☐
Week 11	$77	☐
Week 12	$77	☐
Week 13	$77	☐

Notes: _____
_____
_____

Road to save $ 1,000

In 3 months

3 MONTHS SAVINGS PLAN

Week 1	$77	☐
Week 2	$77	☐
Week 3	$77	☐
Week 4	$77	☐
Week 5	$77	☐
Week 6	$77	☐
Week 7	$77	☐
Week 8	$77	☐
Week 9	$77	☐
Week 10	$77	☐
Week 11	$77	☐
Week 12	$77	☐
Week 13	$77	☐

Notes: _____
_____
_____

Road to save $ 1,000

In 3 months

3 MONTHS SAVINGS PLAN

Week 1	$77	☐
Week 2	$77	☐
Week 3	$77	☐
Week 4	$77	☐
Week 5	$77	☐
Week 6	$77	☐
Week 7	$77	☐
Week 8	$77	☐
Week 9	$77	☐
Week 10	$77	☐
Week 11	$77	☐
Week 12	$77	☐
Week 13	$77	☐

Notes: _____
_____
_____

Road to save $ 1,000

In 3 months

3 MONTHS SAVINGS PLAN

Week 1	$77	☐
Week 2	$77	☐
Week 3	$77	☐
Week 4	$77	☐
Week 5	$77	☐
Week 6	$77	☐
Week 7	$77	☐
Week 8	$77	☐
Week 9	$77	☐
Week 10	$77	☐
Week 11	$77	☐
Week 12	$77	☐
Week 13	$77	☐

Notes:

Road to save $ 1,000

In 3 months

3 MONTHS SAVINGS PLAN

Week 1	$77	☐
Week 2	$77	☐
Week 3	$77	☐
Week 4	$77	☐
Week 5	$77	☐
Week 6	$77	☐
Week 7	$77	☐
Week 8	$77	☐
Week 9	$77	☐
Week 10	$77	☐
Week 11	$77	☐
Week 12	$77	☐
Week 13	$77	☐

Notes: _____
_____
_____
_____

Road to save $ 1,000

In 3 months

3 MONTHS SAVINGS PLAN

Week 1	$77	☐
Week 2	$77	☐
Week 3	$77	☐
Week 4	$77	☐
Week 5	$77	☐
Week 6	$77	☐
Week 7	$77	☐
Week 8	$77	☐
Week 9	$77	☐
Week 10	$77	☐
Week 11	$77	☐
Week 12	$77	☐
Week 13	$77	☐

Notes: _____
_____
_____

Road to save $ 1,000

In 3 months

3 MONTHS SAVINGS PLAN

Week 1	$77	☐
Week 2	$77	☐
Week 3	$77	☐
Week 4	$77	☐
Week 5	$77	☐
Week 6	$77	☐
Week 7	$77	☐
Week 8	$77	☐
Week 9	$77	☐
Week 10	$77	☐
Week 11	$77	☐
Week 12	$77	☐
Week 13	$77	☐

Notes: _____
_____
_____

Road to save $ 1,000

In 3 months

3 MONTHS SAVINGS PLAN

Week 1	$77	☐
Week 2	$77	☐
Week 3	$77	☐
Week 4	$77	☐
Week 5	$77	☐
Week 6	$77	☐
Week 7	$77	☐
Week 8	$77	☐
Week 9	$77	☐
Week 10	$77	☐
Week 11	$77	☐
Week 12	$77	☐
Week 13	$77	☐

Notes: _____
_____
_____

$10,000 In 52 weeks

Savings challenge

$100	$100	$100	$100	$100	$100	$100
$100	$100	$100	$100	$100	$150	$150
$150	$150	$150	$150	$150	$150	$150
$150	$150	$150	$150	$150	$200	$200
$200	$200	$200	$200	$200	$200	$250
$250	$250	$250	$250	$250	$250	$250
$250	$300	$300	$300	$300	$300	$300
$350	$350	$350				

Notes: _____
_____
_____

$10,000 In 52 weeks

Savings challenge

$100	$100	$100	$100	$100	$100	$100
$100	$100	$100	$100	$100	$150	$150
$150	$150	$150	$150	$150	$150	$150
$150	$150	$150	$150	$150	$200	$200
$200	$200	$200	$200	$200	$200	$250
$250	$250	$250	$250	$250	$250	$250
$250	$300	$300	$300	$300	$300	$300
$350	$350	$350				

Notes: _____

_____

_____

$10,000 In 52 weeks

Savings challenge

$100	$100	$100	$100	$100	$100	$100
$100	$100	$100	$100	$100	$150	$150
$150	$150	$150	$150	$150	$150	$150
$150	$150	$150	$150	$150	$200	$200
$200	$200	$200	$200	$200	$200	$250
$250	$250	$250	$250	$250	$250	$250
$250	$300	$300	$300	$300	$300	$300
$350	$350	$350				

Notes:

$10,000 In 52 weeks

Savings challenge

$100	$100	$100	$100	$100	$100	$100
$100	$100	$100	$100	$100	$150	$150
$150	$150	$150	$150	$150	$150	$150
$150	$150	$150	$150	$150	$200	$200
$200	$200	$200	$200	$200	$200	$250
$250	$250	$250	$250	$250	$250	$250
$250	$300	$300	$300	$300	$300	$300
$350	$350	$350				

Notes: _____

_____

_____

$10,000 In 52 weeks

Savings challenge

$100	$100	$100	$100	$100	$100	$100
$100	$100	$100	$100	$100	$150	$150
$150	$150	$150	$150	$150	$150	$150
$150	$150	$150	$150	$150	$200	$200
$200	$200	$200	$200	$200	$200	$250
$250	$250	$250	$250	$250	$250	$250
$250	$300	$300	$300	$300	$300	$300
$350	$350	$350				

Notes: _____

_____

_____

$10,000 In 52 weeks

Savings challenge

$100	$100	$100	$100	$100	$100	$100
$100	$100	$100	$100	$100	$150	$150
$150	$150	$150	$150	$150	$150	$150
$150	$150	$150	$150	$150	$200	$200
$200	$200	$200	$200	$200	$200	$250
$250	$250	$250	$250	$250	$250	$250
$250	$300	$300	$300	$300	$300	$300
$350	$350	$350				

Notes: _____
_____
_____

$10,000 In 52 weeks

Savings challenge

$100	$100	$100	$100	$100	$100	$100
$100	$100	$100	$100	$100	$150	$150
$150	$150	$150	$150	$150	$150	$150
$150	$150	$150	$150	$150	$200	$200
$200	$200	$200	$200	$200	$200	$250
$250	$250	$250	$250	$250	$250	$250
$250	$300	$300	$300	$300	$300	$300
$350	$350	$350				

Notes: _____
_____
_____

$10,000 In 52 weeks

Savings challenge

$100	$100	$100	$100	$100	$100	$100
$100	$100	$100	$100	$100	$150	$150
$150	$150	$150	$150	$150	$150	$150
$150	$150	$150	$150	$150	$200	$200
$200	$200	$200	$200	$200	$200	$250
$250	$250	$250	$250	$250	$250	$250
$250	$300	$300	$300	$300	$300	$300
$350	$350	$350				

Notes: _____
_____
_____

$10,000 In 52 weeks

Savings challenge

$100	$100	$100	$100	$100	$100	$100
$100	$100	$100	$100	$100	$150	$150
$150	$150	$150	$150	$150	$150	$150
$150	$150	$150	$150	$150	$200	$200
$200	$200	$200	$200	$200	$200	$250
$250	$250	$250	$250	$250	$250	$250
$250	$300	$300	$300	$300	$300	$300
$350	$350	$350				

Notes: _____
_____
_____

$10,000 In 52 weeks

Savings challenge

$100	$100	$100	$100	$100	$100	$100
$100	$100	$100	$100	$100	$150	$150
$150	$150	$150	$150	$150	$150	$150
$150	$150	$150	$150	$150	$200	$200
$200	$200	$200	$200	$200	$200	$250
$250	$250	$250	$250	$250	$250	$250
$250	$300	$300	$300	$300	$300	$300
$350	$350	$350				

Notes: _____
_____
_____

$10,000 In 52 weeks

Savings challenge

$100	$100	$100	$100	$100	$100	$100
$100	$100	$100	$100	$100	$150	$150
$150	$150	$150	$150	$150	$150	$150
$150	$150	$150	$150	$150	$200	$200
$200	$200	$200	$200	$200	$200	$250
$250	$250	$250	$250	$250	$250	$250
$250	$300	$300	$300	$300	$300	$300
$350	$350	$350				

Notes:

$10,000 In 52 weeks

Savings challenge

$100	$100	$100	$100	$100	$100	$100
$100	$100	$100	$100	$100	$150	$150
$150	$150	$150	$150	$150	$150	$150
$150	$150	$150	$150	$150	$200	$200
$200	$200	$200	$200	$200	$200	$250
$250	$250	$250	$250	$250	$250	$250
$250	$300	$300	$300	$300	$300	$300
$350	$350	$350				

Notes: _____
_____
_____
_____

$10,000 In 52 weeks

Savings challenge

$100	$100	$100	$100	$100	$100	$100
$100	$100	$100	$100	$100	$150	$150
$150	$150	$150	$150	$150	$150	$150
$150	$150	$150	$150	$150	$200	$200
$200	$200	$200	$200	$200	$200	$250
$250	$250	$250	$250	$250	$250	$250
$250	$300	$300	$300	$300	$300	$300
$350	$350	$350				

Notes: _____
_____
_____

$10,000 In 52 weeks

Savings challenge

$100	$100	$100	$100	$100	$100	$100
$100	$100	$100	$100	$100	$150	$150
$150	$150	$150	$150	$150	$150	$150
$150	$150	$150	$150	$150	$200	$200
$200	$200	$200	$200	$200	$200	$250
$250	$250	$250	$250	$250	$250	$250
$250	$300	$300	$300	$300	$300	$300
$350	$350	$350				

Notes: _____

_____

_____

$10,000 In 52 weeks

Savings challenge

$100	$100	$100	$100	$100	$100	$100
$100	$100	$100	$100	$100	$150	$150
$150	$150	$150	$150	$150	$150	$150
$150	$150	$150	$150	$150	$200	$200
$200	$200	$200	$200	$200	$200	$250
$250	$250	$250	$250	$250	$250	$250
$250	$300	$300	$300	$300	$300	$300
$350	$350	$350				

Notes: _____
_____
_____

$10,000 In 52 weeks

Savings challenge

$100	$100	$100	$100	$100	$100	$100
$100	$100	$100	$100	$100	$150	$150
$150	$150	$150	$150	$150	$150	$150
$150	$150	$150	$150	$150	$200	$200
$200	$200	$200	$200	$200	$200	$250
$250	$250	$250	$250	$250	$250	$250
$250	$300	$300	$300	$300	$300	$300
$350	$350	$350				

Notes: _____
_____
_____

$10,000 In 52 weeks

Savings challenge

$100	$100	$100	$100	$100	$100	$100
$100	$100	$100	$100	$100	$150	$150
$150	$150	$150	$150	$150	$150	$150
$150	$150	$150	$150	$150	$200	$200
$200	$200	$200	$200	$200	$200	$250
$250	$250	$250	$250	$250	$250	$250
$250	$300	$300	$300	$300	$300	$300
$350	$350	$350				

Notes: _____

_____

_____

$10,000 In 52 weeks

Savings challenge

$100	$100	$100	$100	$100	$100	$100
$100	$100	$100	$100	$100	$150	$150
$150	$150	$150	$150	$150	$150	$150
$150	$150	$150	$150	$150	$200	$200
$200	$200	$200	$200	$200	$200	$250
$250	$250	$250	$250	$250	$250	$250
$250	$300	$300	$300	$300	$300	$300
$350	$350	$350				

Notes: _____
_____
_____

$10,000 In 52 weeks

Savings challenge

$100	$100	$100	$100	$100	$100	$100
$100	$100	$100	$100	$100	$150	$150
$150	$150	$150	$150	$150	$150	$150
$150	$150	$150	$150	$150	$200	$200
$200	$200	$200	$200	$200	$200	$250
$250	$250	$250	$250	$250	$250	$250
$250	$300	$300	$300	$300	$300	$300
$350	$350	$350				

Notes: _____

_____

_____

$10,000 In 52 weeks

Savings challenge

$100	$100	$100	$100	$100	$100	$100
$100	$100	$100	$100	$100	$150	$150
$150	$150	$150	$150	$150	$150	$150
$150	$150	$150	$150	$150	$200	$200
$200	$200	$200	$200	$200	$200	$250
$250	$250	$250	$250	$250	$250	$250
$250	$300	$300	$300	$300	$300	$300
$350	$350	$350				

Notes: _____
_____
_____

$10,000 In 52 weeks

Savings challenge

$100	$100	$100	$100	$100	$100	$100
$100	$100	$100	$100	$100	$150	$150
$150	$150	$150	$150	$150	$150	$150
$150	$150	$150	$150	$150	$200	$200
$200	$200	$200	$200	$200	$200	$250
$250	$250	$250	$250	$250	$250	$250
$250	$300	$300	$300	$300	$300	$300
$350	$350	$350				

Notes: _____
_____
_____

$10,000 In 52 weeks

Savings challenge

$100	$100	$100	$100	$100	$100	$100
$100	$100	$100	$100	$100	$150	$150
$150	$150	$150	$150	$150	$150	$150
$150	$150	$150	$150	$150	$200	$200
$200	$200	$200	$200	$200	$200	$250
$250	$250	$250	$250	$250	$250	$250
$250	$300	$300	$300	$300	$300	$300
$350	$350	$350				

Notes:

$10,000 In 52 weeks

Savings challenge

$100	$100	$100	$100	$100	$100	$100
$100	$100	$100	$100	$100	$150	$150
$150	$150	$150	$150	$150	$150	$150
$150	$150	$150	$150	$150	$200	$200
$200	$200	$200	$200	$200	$200	$250
$250	$250	$250	$250	$250	$250	$250
$250	$300	$300	$300	$300	$300	$300
$350	$350	$350				

Notes: _____
_____
_____

$10,000 In 52 weeks

Savings challenge

$100	$100	$100	$100	$100	$100	$100
$100	$100	$100	$100	$100	$150	$150
$150	$150	$150	$150	$150	$150	$150
$150	$150	$150	$150	$150	$200	$200
$200	$200	$200	$200	$200	$200	$250
$250	$250	$250	$250	$250	$250	$250
$250	$300	$300	$300	$300	$300	$300
$350	$350	$350				

Notes: _____
_____
_____

$10,000 In 52 weeks

Savings challenge

$100	$100	$100	$100	$100	$100	$100
$100	$100	$100	$100	$100	$150	$150
$150	$150	$150	$150	$150	$150	$150
$150	$150	$150	$150	$150	$200	$200
$200	$200	$200	$200	$200	$200	$250
$250	$250	$250	$250	$250	$250	$250
$250	$300	$300	$300	$300	$300	$300
$350	$350	$350				

Notes: _____
_____
_____

$10,000 In 52 weeks

Savings challenge

$100	$100	$100	$100	$100	$100	$100
$100	$100	$100	$100	$100	$150	$150
$150	$150	$150	$150	$150	$150	$150
$150	$150	$150	$150	$150	$200	$200
$200	$200	$200	$200	$200	$200	$250
$250	$250	$250	$250	$250	$250	$250
$250	$300	$300	$300	$300	$300	$300
$350	$350	$350				

Notes: _____
_____
_____

$10,000 In 52 weeks

Savings challenge

$100	$100	$100	$100	$100	$100	$100
$100	$100	$100	$100	$100	$150	$150
$150	$150	$150	$150	$150	$150	$150
$150	$150	$150	$150	$150	$200	$200
$200	$200	$200	$200	$200	$200	$250
$250	$250	$250	$250	$250	$250	$250
$250	$300	$300	$300	$300	$300	$300
$350	$350	$350				

Notes: _____
_____
_____

$10,000 In 52 weeks

Savings challenge

$100	$100	$100	$100	$100	$100	$100
$100	$100	$100	$100	$100	$150	$150
$150	$150	$150	$150	$150	$150	$150
$150	$150	$150	$150	$150	$200	$200
$200	$200	$200	$200	$200	$200	$250
$250	$250	$250	$250	$250	$250	$250
$250	$300	$300	$300	$300	$300	$300
$350	$350	$350				

Notes: _____
_____
_____

$10,000 In 52 weeks

Savings challenge

$100	$100	$100	$100	$100	$100	$100
$100	$100	$100	$100	$100	$150	$150
$150	$150	$150	$150	$150	$150	$150
$150	$150	$150	$150	$150	$200	$200
$200	$200	$200	$200	$200	$200	$250
$250	$250	$250	$250	$250	$250	$250
$250	$300	$300	$300	$300	$300	$300
$350	$350	$350				

Notes: _____

_____

_____

$10,000 In 52 weeks

Savings challenge

$100	$100	$100	$100	$100	$100	$100
$100	$100	$100	$100	$100	$150	$150
$150	$150	$150	$150	$150	$150	$150
$150	$150	$150	$150	$150	$200	$200
$200	$200	$200	$200	$200	$200	$250
$250	$250	$250	$250	$250	$250	$250
$250	$300	$300	$300	$300	$300	$300
$350	$350	$350				

Notes: _____
_____
_____

Made in United States
Troutdale, OR
09/26/2023

13192142R00070